LEVEL
III

McMaster
English

Contents

Contents

01

Food and Health

1 Food and Health

I Read the passage and answer questions

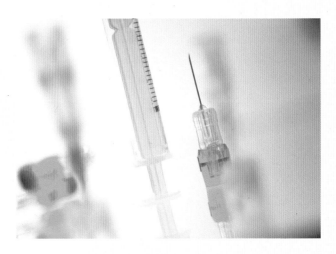

A vaccine is a medicine that prevents a person from getting a certain disease. It is usually a weakened or killed version of a germ that causes the disease. For each disease, the appropriate vaccine is given to people, usually by injection. The vaccine causes substance to be formed in the body and to fight the germ. When the germ gets into the body later again, the remaining substance destroy it.

Vaccines have reduced many diseases that killed or severely disabled people just a few generations ago. For most people today, vaccines are an essential part of healthcare.

1. **What is the main topic of the passage?**

    a. The study of scientists

    b. The function of vaccine

    c. Diseases from vaccines

    d. How to use vaccines

2. **What is the main idea of the passage?**

    a. Scientists are working on vaccines.

    b. A vaccine is a medicine from animals.

    c. A vaccine keeps a person from having a certain illness.

    d. A vaccine is a substance that causes a certain disease.

3. **What is the best title for thee passage?**

    a. What do vaccine do?

    b. Who makes vaccine?

    c. When do people need vaccine?

    d. Why have scientists studied vaccines?

II Write the keyword of the passage

An allergy is the body's abnormally sensitive reaction to some substances. Not everyone has allergies. People who do have allergies may be allergic to one or more things. Dust, animals, plants, bee stings or food are substances that may cause a person to have an allergic reaction. The body mistakenly believes those substances are harmful and it creates specific antibodies to resist them. An allergy is a non-infectious disease and cannot spread to or be caught from other people.

III Write the topic sentence of the passage in English

Secondhand smoking does badly affect people. There are documented studies on the damages of secondhand smoking. The smoke sent out from the smoker is harmful to non-smokers, because it contains nicotine. The smoke includes exhaled smoke as well as smoke from the burning cigarette. People who are exposed to that type of smoke may get more colds and infections than people who are not exposed to it. Non-smokers that have been exposed for a long time can get the same diseases that smokers get. They include even cancer.

SECONDHAND SMOKE is the 3rd leading cause of preventable death in the US.
burlingtonpartnership.org

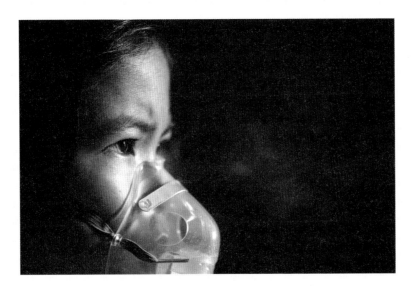

IV Read the passage and answer questions

People have enjoyed many drinks made from plants containing caffeine. Tea, cocoa, and coffee are made from plants that contain caffeine. Caffeine is added to some soft drinks for flavor. It is also included in some food such as chocolate.

Caffeine is a kind of drug found in many different plants. Pure caffeine is a white crystalline powder that has a bitter taste. It speeds up the beating of the heart. A dose of caffeine makes people less tired and more alert. It is often used to stay awake longer. Because of this, a lot of caffeine should be avoided right before going to bed. Scientific research has shown that a moderate amount of caffeine is safe for most adult. Children should not eat or drink too much food and drink that contain caffeine like chocolate, chocolate cookies or cakes, and sodas.

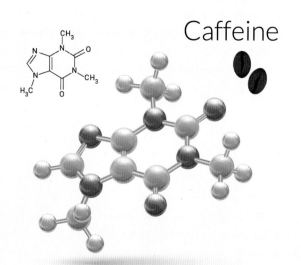

Caffeine

1. What is the main topic of the passage?

    a. Plants containing caffeine

    b. The history of caffeine

    c. The harmfulness of caffeine

    d. The effects of caffeine

2. What is true about caffeine?

    a. Caffeine is the name of a plant.

    b. Caffeine makes people sleep well.

    c. Caffeine is found in chocolate.

    d. Caffeine is important to children.

V Read the passage and answer questions

These days, not a few adults have high cholesterol levels. According to medicine studies, the high level of cholesterol cause

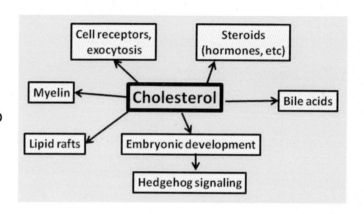

heart disease, which kills many people every year. Therefore, it's often overlooked that cholesterol is vital to human life.

Cholesterol is a white and waxy, fat-like compound. A little amount of cholesterol might feel like a soft melted candle.

Cholesterol is a substance that allows the cells to resist changes in temperature and protects nerve fibers. It helps form some hormones in the body. It is also essential in producing vitamin D in the skin when the body is exposed to sunlight.

The body gets cholesterol in two ways. Some of it is made naturally in the liver and the rest comes from food such as meats, fish, eggs, butter, cheese, and whole milk. Food from plants like fruits, vegetables, and cereals does not have cholesterol.

1. What is the best title for the passage?

    a. What to eat for good health.

    b. What is cholesterol?

    c. Cholesterol, the main cause of heart disease.

    d. Where can we get cholesterol?

2. In which part of the body is some cholesterol naturally made?

    a. Skin

    b. Heart

    c. Cell

    d. Liver

Actual Mini *TOEFL*

Read the paragraph and answer questions.

The food that is taken in the body is **_broken down_** into glucose. It is a type of sugar used for energy. Diabetes is a **_disease_** that prevents the body from metabolizing glucose properly. People with diabetes don't have enough insulin which control

the level of the sugar in their blood. So they have too much sugar in their blood and urine.

There are two types of diabetes, Type 1 and Type 2. Type 1 diabetes happens to children or young adults. They must take insulin through injections because their body either does not make insulin at all, or does not make enough of it. Type 2 diabetes usually develops in people older than 40 or people are very overweight. Type 2 diabetes may develop slowly over time and the symptoms may be mild and often easily overlooked. Type 2 can be **_treated_** by controlling one's lifestyle.

A person who has Type 2 diabetes should eat the same amount of food regularly and avoid certain food including sugar and fat. He should control his weight and maintain it within normal range. Taking medicines or insulin injection should be accompanied with exercise each day.

1. What does the passage mainly discuss?

    a. The food that causes diabetes

    b. How to overcome diabetes

    c. The type of diabetes

    d. The history of diabetes treatment

2. The phrase "broken down" in the passage is opposite in meaning

    to

    a. developed

    b. used

    c. controlled

    d. combined

3. The word "disease" in the passage is closest in meaning to

   a. health

   b. symptom

   c. disorder

   d. possibility

4. What is necessary to control the level of sugar in blood?

   a. Sugar

   b. Insulin

   c. Vitamin

   d. Fat

5. Who has a greater possibility of having Type 2 diabetes?

   a. A child who is shorter than others

   b. A young adult who is taller than others

   c. A 45 years old woman who exercises regularly

   d. A 56 years old man who is overweight

6. What is the word "treated" in the passage is closest in meaning to

    a. cured

    b. applied

    c. added

    d. satisfied

7. Which of the following is helpful for people with diabetes?

    a. Eating enough food

    b. Exercising every morning

    c. Gaining more weight

    d. Drinking coffees at any time

Communication

02

2 Communication

I Write the key words of the passage

A cellular phone is a type of wireless communication. A cellular phone is called "cell-phone" because the system uses many base station to divide a service  area into multiple cells. Each cell has a central base station and uses frequencies different from those used by the nearby cells.

The basic concept of cellular phones began in the late 1940s in Britain and America. Researchers came up with an idea of a cellular phone by studying police mobile car phones. However, the computer technology just was not developed enough to achieve this idea at that time.

II Write the topic sentence of the passage

The Internet is a very useful communication system. The global Internet today offers much more diverse tools and context for communication than it offered in the past.

People on the earth can read the same news and debate the same topic on the Web wherever they live. Producers can give information about new products to consumers and consumers can order products on the Internet. The Internet enables more and more people to interact together. The impact of the Internet on human communication can be compared to a revolution.

_____

III **Read the passage and answer questions.**

America's first independent newspaper was published by James Franklin in 1721. It was the *New England Courant*. After the Revolutionary War started in  1775, more independent newspapers were published to inform the colonists of news. There are 40 different kinds of newspapers at that time and many of them were weeklies or monthlies.

During the 1780s and 1790s, citizens relied on the press more to keep up with political changes in the country. This caused the publication of the daily newspaper. America's first daily newspaper, *The Pennsylvania Packet and Daily Advertiser*, began publication in Philadelphia in 1784. *The New York Post* is the oldest newspaper in the USA with a continuous daily publication.

Today, there are many other American newspapers such as the *New York Daily News* and the *Washington Post*. Some newspapers are issued in other languages except in English.

1. What does the passage mainly discuss?

   a. Brief history of America's newspapers

   b. America's first newspaper

   c. America's political change

   d. Two main newspapers in colonial America

2. When was America's first daily newspaper published?

   a. By the start of Revolutionary War

   b. In 1721

   c. In the 1780s

   d. After the publication of the Washington Post

IV Read the passage and answer questions.

An art professor Samuel F. B. Morse thought of a new communication system. It was to transmit messages by using an electro-magnet which was  activated by alternately making and breaking the electric circuit. The messages were passed through a network of telegraph stations. In order to transmit messages in this system, Morse invented the Morse Code, an alphabet of electronic dots and dashes. He sent an experimental message from Washington D.C to Baltimore on May 24, 1844. The success of experiment made communications across the country faster than ever before.

The first transcontinental telegraph line in America was completed in 1861. Because of the telegraph system, the Pony Express that delivered mail through horses and riders was doomed to disappear into history books. People sent telegrams to announce important news such as a new birth or a death in the family. During the Civil War, the telegraph made it possible to connect the scattered military units.

1. What is the main idea of the paragraph 1?

    a. Morse was interested in art.

    b. People sent telegram to give information.

    c. Morse invented the telegraph system.

    d. People communicated with others through telegrams.

2. How did the Pony Express deliver mail?

    a. By car

    b. Through horses and riders

    c. Through telegraph stations

    d. By military units

V Read the passage and answer questions.

Today, digital voice and computer data are transmitted at the speed of light through glass fibers called optical fibers. This was possible by putting Bell's photo phone into practice.

Alexander Graham Bell, who invented the telephone, also invented the photo phone. While a telephone used electricity for voice communication, the photo phone was based on transmitting sound on a beam of light. The vibrations of a person's voice projected on a mirror caused similar vibrations in the mirror. Sunlight projected the vibrations back to the photophone's receiver. There the vibrations were converted back into sound.

It took a long time before Bell's idea became practical. The original machine had a big flaw that it could work only when the weather was sunny. Nevertheless, Bell's photophone was one of the most important inventions that made optical communications possible.

1. What is the best title for the passage?

    a. Who invented the photophone?

    b. The invention of telephone

    c. Brief history of communication

    d. A basis for optical communications, Bell's photophone

2. What weather was the best for the first photophone?

    a. Sunny weather

    b. Cloudy weather

    c. Rainy weather

    d. Windy weather

Actual Mini TOEFL

Read the paragraph and answer questions.

One of the most important means of communication through pictures and sound is the television. By watching TV, people learn about the world and their surrounding neighbors.

The first television sets were not entirely electronic. These TV sets used a small motor to rotate a disk to produce a picture. A neon lamp behind a disk worked together to give the picture. The period before 1935 is called *Mechanical Television Era*.

The picture quality of mechanical televisions was very poor. The screens were about half the size of the business card and it was made up of only 30 to 60 screen lines. The number of lines was very small, compared with the present *system* with 525 lines.

It was John Logie Baird, a Scottish engineer, who accomplished the first transmission of simple face shapes by using mechanical television. He publicly demonstrated the television several times. With his transmitting equipment, the BBC first *broadcast* the regularly scheduled television program in September of 1929. In the United States, television was being broadcast from over a dozen stations by 1930.

1. What is the author's main point in the passage?

    a. The first type of the television

    b. Invention of the television

    c. The principle of the television

    d. The use of the television

2. What was the motor in the first television set used for?

    a. It powered television.

    b. It made the picture colorful.

    c. It made sound.

    d. It rotated a disk.

3. What is the main idea of paragraph 3?

   a. The first television had 30 screen lines.

   b. The picture and screen of the mechanical television was poor.

   c. The first television produced a clear picture.

   d. Today's televisions are better than the first television.

4. What is the word "system" in the passage closest in meaning to

   a. motor

   b. disk

   c. television

   d. station

5. What is not true about John Logie Baired?

   a. He was an engineer.

   b. With his television, the United States began broadcasting.

   c. He first achieved the transmission of face shapes.

   d. He demonstrated the mechanical television to the public.

6. The word "broadcast" in the passage is closest in meaning to

   a. aired

   b. gave

   c. brought

   d. sent

7. How many broadcasting stations were there in the United States

   by 1930?

   a. Only one

   b. More than twelve

   c. 30 to 60

   d. About a hundred

03

Sports and Athletes

3 Sports and Athletes

I Write the key words of the passage.

From 1940 to 1953, Ben Hogan won every major championship available as a professional golfer. He took the US Open four times, the PGA twice and the British Open the only time

he played in. In his last great year, 1953, Ben Hogan won the US and British Opens and the Masters, three-quarters of what is now considered the Grand Slam of Professional golf. Even though Ben Hogan era ended, the stimulation and attraction that he gave to people did not recede.

_____

Write the topic sentence of the passage.

    Soccer is a sport in which players kick a ball on a field. Many ancient cultures played a sport similar to modern soccer. The Munich Museum in Germany has an ancient Chinese text that mentions games very similar to soccer. The Chinese made a leather ball and filled it with hair. The ancient Romans played a game similar to soccer so vigorously that two-thirds of the players were injured during the game.

_____

III Read the passage and answer questions.

In the early days in the history of baseball, there were several variations of the game known as "rounders" or "four-old-cat." At that time, the game had no official rules. People decided their own rules when they played the game. Rounders had many of the same features as baseball has today.

Baseball became an organized sport in the 1840s and 1850s. Many early baseball teams were formed in New York City and Brooklyn. By 1860, baseball became America's most popular game. Although there were many teams in New York, baseball was an amateur sport, which meant that players were not paid to play.

The first professional baseball team was the Cincinnati Red Stockings. Harry Wright, the Reds' player-manager, is known as the "Father of Professional Baseball." Although the National Association didn't want to support the professional baseball movement, Major League Baseball in America had begun.

1. What is the main topic of the passage?

    a. History of baseball

    b. The rules of baseball

    c. The development of professional baseball

    d. Famous baseball players

2. According to the passage, who was Harry Wright?

    a. The mayor of Cincinnati

    b. A Major League Baseball player

    c. A member of the national association

    d. A manager of the first professional baseball team

IV Read the passage and answer questions.

Tennis is a game enjoyed by millions all over the world. Outstanding players are loved by many tennis fans. Monica Seles is one of them.

Monica Seles was born in Yugoslavia. Her elder brother Zoltan taught tennis to her. At the age of nine, she won the Yugoslavian championship for 12 and under. When she was eleven, she met the legendary coach Nick Bolletieri and was trained at his tennis academy. She made her debut as a professional in 1989. Soon she became one of the top tennis players in the world.

In 1993, Monica was tragically stabbed by an insane fan of Steffi Graf. Monica was injured and it took a long time for her to recover from the attack. She made her comeback to the tennis court on July 29, 1995. Then she triumphed by winning a match against Steffi Graf in January, 1996. The hardship she had to endure made her a more distinguished player.

1. What is the best title for the passage?

   a. Tennis player, Steffi Graf

   b. A favorite sport, tennis

   c. An outstanding tennis player, Monica Seles

   d. Monica Seles' tragedy

2. Who introduced tennis to Monica Seles?

   a. Her brother

   b. Nick Bollitieri

   c. A fan of Steffi Graf

   d. Steffi Graf

V Read the passage and answer questions.

One of the most demanding but graceful sports is gymnasium. Precision, control, speed, strength, concentration, and discipline are required for gymnastics. The

first gymnastics was circus-like acrobatics in ancient Egypt. The ancient Greeks developed gymnastics as an exercise for the maintenance of good physical condition. They believed that gymnastics could change the mind and body. For many successive centuries, acrobats and dancers performed movements similar to the ones we see in today's gymnastics.

F. I. Jahn, an educator, opened an outdoor gymnasium near Berlin in 1881. He was the first person to use the bars. He also developed the horse and the rings. P. H. Ling is another person who developed gymnastics. While Jahn emphasized self-discipline and physical strength, Ling concentrated on freedom of movement and free expression.

1. What is the main idea of paragraph 2?

    a. Jahn and Ling developed modern gymnastics.

    b. Many gymnasiums were opened in the nineteen century.

    c. There are many kinds of gymnastics.

    d. Jahn used gymnastics for training athletes.

2. What did the Ancient Greeks do to maintain good physical condition?

    a. They danced at the ball.

    b. They practiced gymnastics.

    c. They took military training.

    d. They became a member of the circus.

Actual Mini *TOEFL*

Read the paragraph and answer questions.

Jackie Robinson, who broke the color barrier in American sports, grew up in California in the 1930s. In those days, African-American were not allowed to play at the youth club because of the color of their skin. Jackie could practice only one day a week. He was an **_outstanding_** player in basketball, baseball, football, track at UCLA.

When Jackie played for the Kansas City Monarchs, a Negro League ball club, Branch Rickey offered him a job as a major league player. He believed that Jackie, no matter what color of his skin was, was good enough to play on a major league team. He also believed that Jackie had the courage and strength to withstand all difficulties.

Jackie Robinson took his new job very **_seriously_**. When other people yelled at him, he dreamed that other African-Americans would follow him into the major league. He quietly showed that he was a good player. Soon he was regarded as one of the best players in his team, and other African-American were allowed to join the major league.

Owing to his courage, today's many black athletes can play with white athletes. Every athlete and every sports fan today appreciate Jackie Robinson' courage.

1. What is the main idea of the passage?

    a. African-Americans believed Jackie Robinson was a good player.

    b. Jackie Robinson broke the barrier of color in American sports.

    c. Jackie Robinson was the best player in American Sports.

    d. The first major league team in American baseball was courageous.

2. Why did Jackie Robinson play at the youth club only once a week?

    a. His parents wanted him to study.

    b. He was too weak to play every day.

    c. He was not allowed to use the youth club every day.

    d. He did not have many friends to play with.

3. The word "outstanding" in the passage is closest in meaning to

    a. remarkable

    b. ordinary

    c. poor

    d. courageous

4. What is true about Branch Rickey?

    a. He was an African-American athlete.

    b. He played on a major league team.

    c. He chose Jackie as a major league player.

    d. He believed that Jackie could break the record.

5. The word "seriously" in the passage is opposite in meaning to

    a. sincerely

    b. happily

    c. unpleasantly

    d. carelessly

6. What did Jackie Robinson do when people made fun of him?

    a. He smiled at him.

    b. He showed his anger to them.

    c. He tried to show his ability as a player.

    d. He appealed to people's emotion.

7. The phrase "owing to" in the passage is closest in meaning to

    a. in order to

    b. on account of

    c. in fact

    d. as a result of

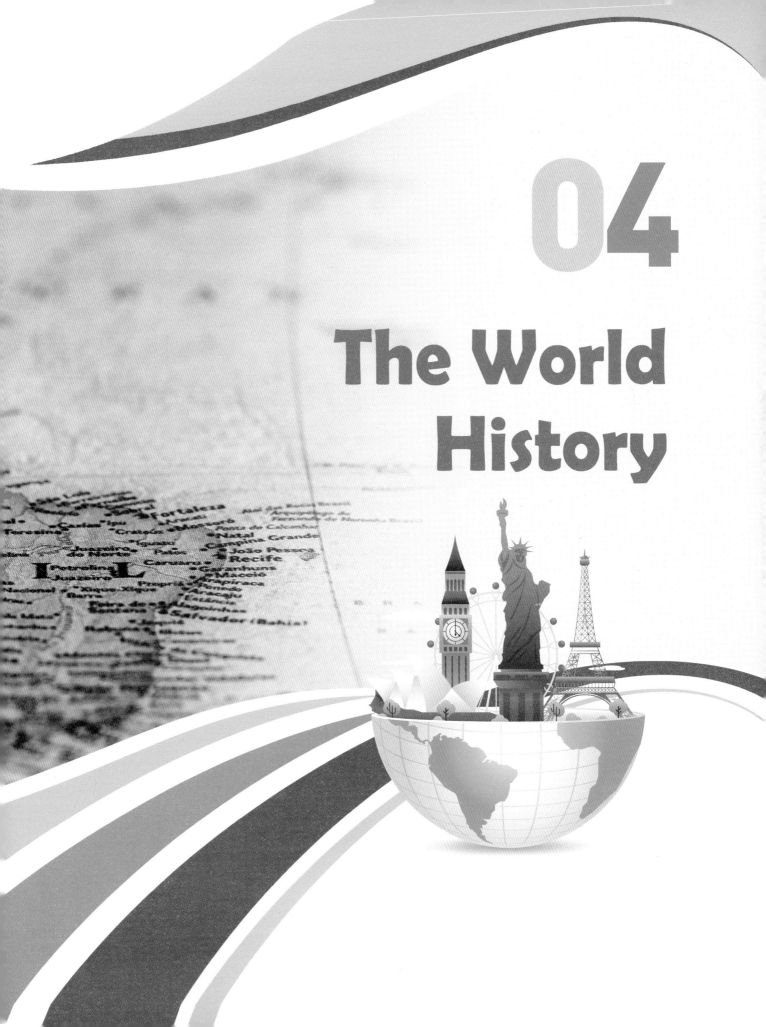

04
The World History

4 The World History

I According to the passage write the answer to the question.

Africa was the stage for the dawn of human history. From about five million years ago, Australopithecus, an intermediate species between apes and men, walked on two feet in this continent. Later, the first creatures to be classed as the human species evolved in Africa. They developed tools and introduced the Stone Age. They left rock and cave paintings in widely separated areas.

What is the creature described to be as an intermediate between apes and men?

_____

II According to the passage, correct the following sentence.

The European Union(EU) is an organization of 25 European countries. The member states cooperate in many areas including politics and economy. The EU has

evolved from economic cooperation that began among Western European countries in the early 1950s. It is a major economic unit in the world. Its members have more people than in the United States. In addition, the combined value of the union's imports and exports is greater than that of any single country in the world.

The members of the EU cooperate only in politics and economics.

_____

III   Read the passage and answer questions.

An Afghanistan, the crossroads of Central Asia, has a violent history. In 328 B.C., Alexander the Great entered the territory of present-day Afghanistan. Invasions by Huns and Turks followed in succeeding centuries. In 642 A.D., Arabs invaded the entire region and introduced Islam to the country. In 1219, the country was invaded by Mongolians led by Genghiskhan. They destroyed many cities and fertile farm land.

The beginning of modern Afghanistan can be traced to 1747 when Ahmad Shah Durrani established his rule. Durrani was elected king by a tribal council after the assassination of Nasir Shah, the Persian ruler. Throughout his reign, Durrani united fragmented provinces into one country. His rule extended and protected the country's boundary.

1. What was the outcome of the Mongolian invasion in Afghanistan?

    a. The Islam Empire was established in the country.

    b. Many parts of the country were destroyed.

    c. Islam was introduced into the country.

    d. The country extended its territory.

2. Which of the following people did not invade Afghanistan?

    a. Persians

    b. Mongols

    c. Israel

    d. Turks

IV Read the passage and answer questions.

From 1740 to 1820, Ireland enjoyed a period of prosperity. Agricultural production increased and the British demanded large

amounts of grain. The population began to soar and reached to 8 million. However, the soil had been depleted and the potato crops failed because of the potato rot. A few years of failure of the crop resulted in the Irish Famine.

The Irish Famine of 1846 and 1850 took as many as one million lives from hunger and disease, and changed the social and cultural structure of Ireland. The Famine also resulted in the dramatic waves of emigration in history. More than a million people emigrated to Britain, the United States, and Australia. Many farmers were driven penniless from their homes. After the Famine, Ireland's population dropped to 5 million. The Famine also changed old agricultural practices that they had relied on being only potato crop.

1. Why did many Irish emigration in the 19th century?

    a. Because of political change

    b. Because of the Famine

    c. Because of the cold weather

    d. Because of overpopulation

2. All of the following are true about the Irish Famine except

    a. It was an agricultural movement.

    b. It caused the decrease of population.

    c. It happened in the mid 19th century.

    d. It resulted from agricultural failure.

V **Read the passage and answer questions.**

Thousands of Loyalists, who had taken Britain's side in the American Revolution, were expelled from the newly independent United States. Some returned to England, but most fled northward into Canada. In the years up to 1783, about 40,000 moved into Canada. Many of them went to Nova Scotia where there had been a British presence for several decades. About 10,000 chose the province of Quebec. By 1784, because of a sudden increase of Loyalists, Nova Scotia was divided into three separate colonies. New Brunswick and Cape Breton were created.

The Canadian constitutional Act of 1791 brought about more significant changes in Canada. This divided Quebec into Upper Canada and Lower Canada. Upper Canada was comprised mostly of English-speaking Loyalists. Lower Canada was inhabited by many French-speaking people.

1. According to the passage, what caused the sudden increase of population in Canada?

    a. American independence

    b. Abundant crops and food

    c. A war in Britain

    d. The Canadian Constitutional Act

2. Which of the following is not true about the Loyalists?

    a. They were loyal to Britain during the American Revolution.

    b. They were expelled from the United States.

    c. They discovered western Canada.

    d. Some of them moved to Quebec.

Actual Mini *TOEFL*

Read the following passage and answer questions.

Democracy is an opposite system of monarchy, in which a single person *<u>rules</u>*. Democracy theoretically means that every adult has the right to influence group decisions. However, even in Athens, where *<u>sophisticated</u>* democracy began, ideal democracy was not practiced.

Athenian democracy in the 5th century B.C. was direct democracy. But in the strict sense, the Athenian democracy was the citizen's democracy. Only certain citizens could participate in voting. They were males, over the age of eighteen, who were sons of Athenian fathers. They formed at most 20% of the whole population that included free women, children and slaves.

Direct democracy has two preconditions. The community must be small enough for citizens to be able to *<u>attend</u>* debates and to vote on issues. And the citizens must have enough leisure to engage in politics. Athens met both circumstances at the time. Even though the Athens democracy was copied by Greek and colonies of Athens, it has rarely been attempted elsewhere. The representative democracy of modern societies is the alternative form of it.

1. What is the main topic of the passage?

    a. The history of monarchy

    b. The history of Athens

    c. The difficulty of democracy

    d. Athenian democracy

2. What is the opposite political system of democracy?

    a. Monarchy

    b. Direct democracy

    c. Citizen democracy

    d. Representative democracy

3. The word "rules" in the passage
    is closest in meaning to

    a. confuses

    b. controls

    c. collides

    d. watches

4. The world "sophisticated" in the passage is opposite in meaning

   to

   a. uncivilized

   b. undiscovered

   c. developed

   d. satisfied

5. Which of the following is true about democracy in Athens of the

   5th Century B.C.?

   a. It was not direct democracy.

   b. Every single person had the right to vote.

   c. Women and slaves were not included as citizens.

   d. The citizens were males and females.

6. All of the following describe Athenian democracy except

    a. It is an ideal democracy.

    b. It reguests citizens to debate and vote on issues.

    c. It is possible in countries where people have enough leisure.

    d. It was once practiced in Greece.

7. The word "attend" in the passage is closest in meaning to

    a. announce

    b. be absent

    c. pretend to

    d. participate in

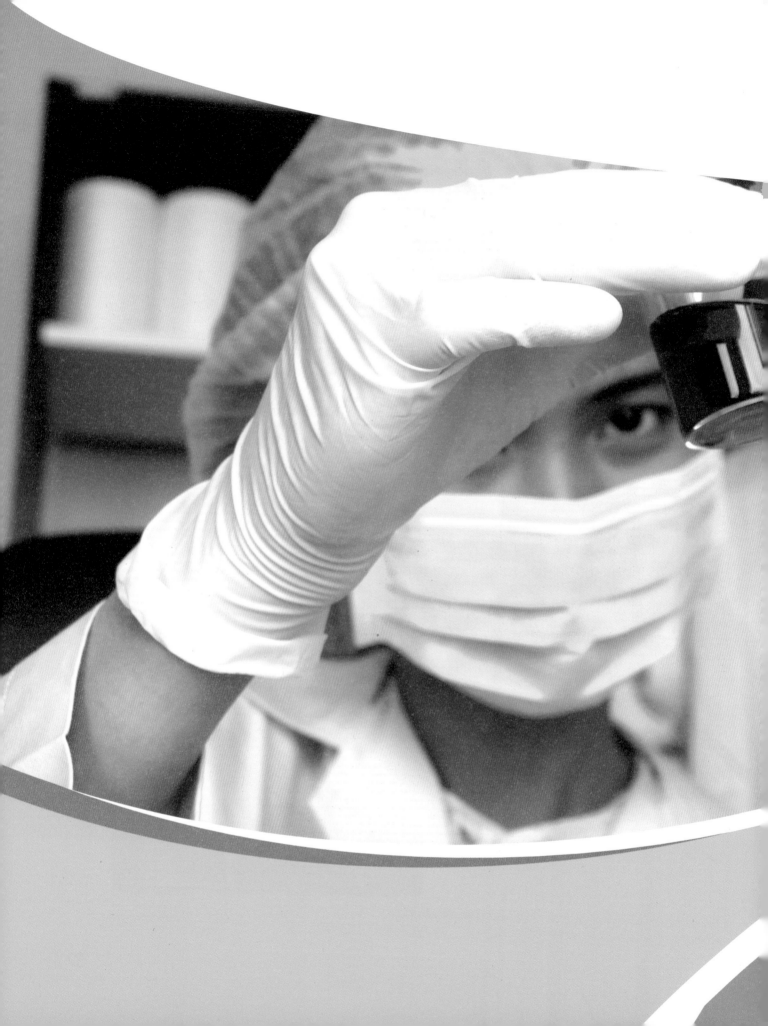

05

Scientists and Inventions

5 Scientists and Inventions

I According to the passage, write the answer to the question.

Marie Curie was the first person to win two Nobel Prizes. She discovered the radioactive elements, polonium, and radium. She believed that the quickest way to a progressive future was to foster research and found the Radium Institute. In 1920, she created the Curie Foundation in order to support the scientific and medical divisions of the Radium Institute. Under her directions, scientists at the Radium Institute published 483 papers and books.

Why did Marie Curie create the Curie Foundation?

_____

II **According to the passage, correct the following sentence.**

Thomas Edison had patent for 1,093 different inventions. Many of them, like the light bulb and the phonograph, were successful creations that influence our everyday life today.

He founded a cement company, but the idea was not accepted because concrete was expensive. The greatest failure of Edison's career was a mining business in his old age. He lost all the money he had invested.

The invention of the light bulb made Edison lose all his money.

_____

III Read the passage and answer questions.

James Watt, the son of
a carpenter, started his
career as an engineer.
In 1763, he was sent a
steam engine for repair.
While repairing it, Watt
discovered how he could
make the engine more
efficient. As a result of

working on the idea, he produced a steam engine that cooled
the used steam. Matthew Boulton, a successful businessman,
provided financial backing for Watt's project. His machine was
very powerful and became very popular. Watt continued to
experiment and produced more advanced types of machinery.
This new engine could be used to drive many types of machinery.
His new machines were used in many of Britain's mines and
factories. Each company saved costs by using his machine rather
than a team of horses. His machine made James Watt a very
wealthy man.

1. **When did Watt come up with the idea of his machine?**

    a. When he got a job as an engineer

    b. When he repaired a steam engine

    c. When he met Matthew Boulton

    d. When he visited a mine

2. **Which of the following is not true about Watt's machine?**

    a. It was a steam engine.

    b. It moved by a team of horse.

    c. It was mainly used in mines and factories.

    d. It made Watt very rich.

Alice Hamilton was born in New York in 1869 and grew up in Indiana. She got her medical degree from the University of Michigan and then attended universities in Munich and Leipzig in Germany for a year. She became  the first woman on the faculty on Harvard University.

She established medical education classes and a well-baby clinic. She spent time investigating lead poisoning among bathtub workers. This resulted in a series of reforms to reduce occupational exposure to lead. She also studied carbon poisoning in steel workers and mercury poisoning in hat makers.

On the basis of her work, more researchers continued to reduce work-related illness and injuries and provided safe and healthy working conditions for men and women.

1. What did Alice Hamilton mainly work on?

    a. Work-related illness

    b. Medical education

    c. Occupational character

    d. Female medicine

2. All of the following are true about Alice Hamilton except

    a. She attended universities in Germany.

    b. She was the first medical professor of Harvard University.

    c. She investigated the relation between illness and job.

    d. She influenced working conditions for many people.

V Read the passage and answer questions.

The invention of the radio had a great influence on today's daily life. The invention was actually made by Alexander Popov, a Russian scientist.

Popov studied physics and mathematics in Sankt-Peterburgh University. Later he became a professor of physics and spent time experimenting electronic technology. One day he was inspired to study wireless connections among ships. After his continuous efforts, he developed the first radio-receiver that could register thunderstorm electricity discharges from considerable distance. In the spring of 1897, Popov conducted some experiments that transmitted information to a ship that was as far as 640 meters from Popov.

His great invention was used for the first time when a ship got stuck in a rock and was in danger. Signals were sent to other ships and they came and helped the ship.

1. According to the passage, what did Popov teach at the university?

    a. Mathematics

    b. Physics

    c. Natural science

    d. Naval investigation

2. Which of the following is not true about the radio?

    a. It was invented by a Russian scientist.

    b. It was used for the first time for a ship in danger.

    c. It has influenced many people's lives.

    d. It was widely used in the early 1800s.

Actual Mini **TOEFL**

Read the following passage and answer questions.

Philip Emeagwali, a Nigerian-born computer scientist, developed supercomputers and the Internet using his mathematics and computer _**expertise**_.

In 1974, he read a science fiction story on how to use 64,000 mathematicians to forecast the weather for the whole Earth. Inspired by that story, he studied a way to use 64,000 processors that would be evenly distributed around the Earth to forecast the weather. He called it a hyperball international network of computers and now we call it the Internet.

He used 65,000 separate computer processors to _**perform**_ 3.1 billion calculations per second in 1989. _**That feat**_ led to computer scientists understanding the capabilities of duper computers and the _**practical**_ applications of creating a system that allowed multiple computers to communicate.

For his contributions, he was voted one of the twenty innovators of the Internet, and he is recognized as "a Father of the Internet."

1. What is the main idea of the passage?

    a. Philip Emeagwali contributed to the development of the Internet.

    b. Philip Emeagwali was a great mathematician.

    c. Philip Emeagwali had difficulty inventing the supercomputer.

    d. Philip Emeagwali is an example of a computer genius.

2. The word "expertise" in the passage is closest in meaning to

    a. experience

    b. interest

    c. know-how

    d. hobby

3. What inspired Emeagwali to think of hyperball?

    a. A science fiction story

    b. His friend

    c. A mathematician

    d. The errors in his computer

4. The word "perform" in the passage is closest in meaning to

    a. hinder

    b. represent

    c. pretend

    d. execute

5. What does the phrase "That feat" in the passage refer to?

    a. Weather forecast using 64,000 mathematicians

    b. His calculations using 65,000 processors

    c. Voting twenty greatest innovators of the Internet

    d. His studies in physics

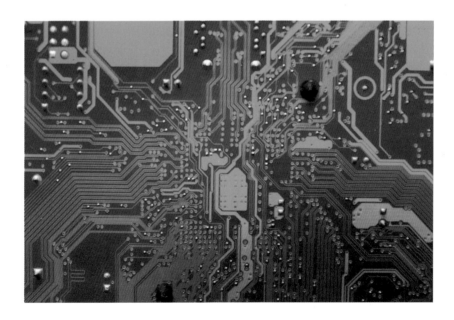

6. The word "practical" in the passage is opposite in meaning to

    a. suitable

    b. ideal

    c. wrong

    d. realistic

7. Which of the following statement about Emeagwali is not

   Supported by the passage?

    a. He stuck to his studies.

    b. He was excellent in mathematics.

    c. He owned a company producing supercomputers.

    d. He is known as "a Father of the Internet".

06

Architecture

6 Architecture

I **According to the passage, write the answer to the questions.**

Antonio Gaudi was an architect in Spain in the late nineteenth and early twentieth centuries. He was in the forefront of the Art Nouveau movement in Spain. His work in

Barcelona created some of the most notable landmarks.

Gaudi was a pioneer in architecture using color, texture, and movement in ways never before imagined. He favored soft and fluid forms versus sharp and angular forms. His works stand as a testimony to his genius.

What kind of forms did Gaudi prefer using in his architecture?

_____

_____

II   According to the passage, correct the following sentence.

Todaiji, a Buddhist temple in Nara, Japan, is the largest human-made wooden structure. There are no screws, nails or glue used in the construction  of this temple. It was first built in 751 but today's temple was rebuilt right after World War II.

When Japan was involved in the war, the Japanese decided to disassemble the temple to protect it from bombs. They loaded the pieces of wood onto railroad tracks that they built up to the structure, and they stored all of the pieces until they could rebuild the temple safely.

Todaiji Temple in Japan was made up of stones.

III Read the passage and answer questions.

Stone is a great material used in construction. It has been used by many architects over a long period of time. The Pyramids of ancient Egypt as well as the Chicago Water Tower are made of stone. Mayan cities had many stone structures built for the rulers and priests.

There are apparent reasons why stone has been used in construction even though it is bulky and hard to move. First, stone is all over the world. It is easily obtained anywhere. Second, stone stays the same color, even under the bright sun or under the pouring rainfall. It is also fireproof and soundproof. Third, stone costs less than other materials because it lasts very long, is durable and does not need painting or refinishing. Above all the most persuasive reason is that stone is really beautiful.

1. Who were the most stone structures in Mayan cities for?

    a. Ancestors

    b. Beautiful women

    c. Poor children

    d. Kings and priests

2. All of the following are merits of stone as a material excepts

    a. It lasts very long.

    b. It is very heavy.

    c. It can withstand fire and various weather condition.

    d. It looks beautiful.

IV Read the passage and answer questions.

Skyscrapers could not have been built without Elisha Graves Otis' invention, an elevator. Otis opened a small factory to make elevators in Yonkers, New York, on September 20, 1853. His elevators were fully equipped with his newly invented automatic safety device.

For six months, he had received only one order to build two freight elevators. Otis staged a public demonstration to show the safety of his invention at the Crystal Palace at the New York Exhibition. He climbed top of his elevator, and ordered the rope cut. People noticed that the safety brake kept him from falling. The performance launched the passenger elevator industry. The world's first safety elevator for passengers was installed in a New York store in 1857.

Without the introduction of steel frame construction, the skyscraper was impossible. With the construction of new and taller buildings, business at the Otis Elevator Company rose steadily.

1. What did Elisha Otis do in the fall of 1853?

    a. He introduced the safety elevator in public

    b. He invented an automatic safety device

    c. He climbed the highest building in New York

    d. He launched an elevator company

2. Which of the following is not true about Otis' elevator?

    a. It was equipped with an automatic safety device

    b. It was first used for freight

    c. It was believed to be safe from the beginning

    d. It made skyscrapers in the world possible

V Read the passage and answer questions.

A geodesic dome is a structure that is shaped like a sphere or a ball. It is composed of a complex network of triangles and is the lightest, strongest, and most cost-effective structure ever devised.

Buckminster Fuller, an architect, invented the geodesic dome in the late 1940s. His lifelong goal was to solve human's major problems through the highest technology by providing more and more life support for everybody, with less and less resources. He had many ideas on how to make buildings cheaper to build using materials and techniques in non-traditional ways.

The geodesic dome is able to cover more space without internal supports than any other enclosure. The geodesic dome is a breakthrough in building, not only in cost-effectiveness, but also in ease of construction. In 1957, a geodesic dome auditorium in Honolulu was put up in 22 hours after the parts were delivered.

1. Why did Fuller try to develop building technology?

    a. To win a prize for architecture

    b. To build as many as possible in his time

    c. To save the cost of constructing buildings

    d. To find the most beautiful structure

2. Which of the following is not true about the geodesic dome?

    a. It was invented by a scientist.

    b. It is the most cost-effective structure.

    c. It can be put up in a short period.

    d. It is non-traditional way to build.

Actual Mini *TOEFL*

Read the following passage and answer questions.

While most American architects in the early 1900s were merely imitating European styles, Frank Lloyd Wright was willing to look to various cultures for inspiration and developed a _unique_ style. He found more inspiration in Japanese design and art and collected exhibitions of Japanese art. Japanese people also understood and appreciated his work.

The Imperial Hotel in Tokyo, Japan was one of Wright's grandest and most elegant works. It was designed in 1915. A few years later when an earthquake hit the region and _destroyed_ many buildings, the hotel was hardly damaged. Many people who did not know of him or his work began to notice him and to request him to design buildings.

Wright believed that good design makes people well aware and respectful of their _surroundings_ and of nature. He designed about 800 buildings. Quite number of them were designed before someone asked him to design. Three hundred eighty of them were built and about 280 are still standing. Frank Lloyd Wright had a strong influence on American architecture.

1. What is the main topic of the passage?

    a. The history of architecture

    b. The difference between American and European styles

    c. The popularity of Wright's design

    d. The originality of Wright's works.

2. What did most American architects study in the early 1900s?

    a. The nature of their country

    b. European buildings

    c. Ancient Greek architects

    d. Japanese design and art

3. The word "unique" in the passage

    is opposite in meaning to

    a. common

    b. original

    c. single

    d. outstanding

4. According to the passage, which of the following is not true about the Imperial Hotel?

   a. It was designed by Frank Lloyd Wright.

   b. It stands in Tokyo, Japan.

   c. It was mostly destroyed by an earthquake.

   d. It made many people ask Wright to design for them.

5. The word "destroyed" in the passage is closest in meaning to

   a. demonstrated

   b. ruined

   c. copied

   d. replied

6. The word "surroundings" in the passage is closest in meaning to

    a. background

    b. stage

    c. environment

    d. scream

7. How many buildings that Wright designed were actually built?

    a. 800 buildings

    b. 380 buildings

    c. 280 buildings

    d. A few buildings

07

Literature

7 Literature

I Write the word that is closest in meaning to "<u>made use of</u>."

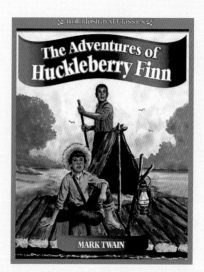

The Adventures of Huckleberry Finn, published in 1885, is considered to be a great American novel by most people. The novel has been read steadily since it was written by Mark Twain. The story is about Huck Finn who helps a slave named Jim to escape along the Mississippi River.

Twain <u>*made use of*</u> humor and irony in expressing justice, and morality. Each character has a unique personality. Twain brought the characters to life by using accents and slang words. So, the dialogues by his characters make them seem to be real people.

_____

II **Write the word that is opposite in meaning to "<u>vague.</u>"**

Modernism was the most remarkable artistic movement of the twentieth century and the most difficult to define. The chief writers associated with the movement were T. S. Eliot, James Joyce, Virginia Woolf, and Ezra Pound. They presented a pessimistic view of culture in disarray unlike the

'THE **MEN** of **1914**' **T.S. ELIOT and early Modernism**

Erik Svarny

nineteenth-century optimism. They didn't use the conventional way of cause and effect development in their works. They used foreign languages and quotations. Their writings were ironic and *vague* in purpose and plot.

III Read the passage and answer questions.

Langston Hughes was one of America's greatest poets. In addition to his work as a poet, Hughes wrote many works as a novelist, columnist, playwright, and essayist. Like many other writers, he wrote about the people, places, and events around him. He used dialects and jazz rhythms in his writings. Most of his

works were closely associated with Harlem. Hughes praised its people because they appreciated the beauty that existed in their lives. He also could make them cheerful. He loved their music, especially the blues. The blues expressed the feelings of people who determined to overcome their _hardships._

He traveled other countries and learned how they dealt with racial issues. His world travel influenced his writings in a profound way. His long and distinguished career produced volumes of diverse genres and inspired the works of countless other African-American writers.

1. The word "hardships" in the passage is closest in meaning to

   a. poverty

   b. sickness

   c. difficulties

   d. luck

2. Which of the following is not related with Langston Hughes?

   a. He was an American poet.

   b. He influenced many British writers.

   c. He traveled many places around the world.

   d. He wrote essays as well as poems.

IV Read the passage and answer questions.

In ancient Egypt, fragmentary papyri represented literature and they were considered as books. The Egyptian and the Greek literary works were usually  written on papyrus. In medieval Europe, books were written on parchment. People took very good care of books. Sometimes books were chained to the tables so no one could steal them.

In early medieval Europe, there were a lot of people writing books. Some books were about the Christian faith. Other books dealt with the history of various countries and people's. Most of them were written in Latin.

In the late Middle Ages, people gradually wrote books in languages that they really spoke instead of in Latin. It enabled more people to read books and to _**acquire**_ knowledge. Books about various themes such as medicine, philosophy, and travel were written in many countries. After the Renaissance, a great number of new books were written.

1. Which of the following is closest in meaning to the word

   "acquire"in the passage?

   a. give

   b. admit

   c. loss

   d. get

2. What did some people in early medieval Europe write about?

   a. Christian faith

   b. Medicine

   c. Philosophy

   d. Art

V Read the passage and answer questions.

Novelist William Faulkner was born in New Albany, Mississippi, on September 25, 1897. He lived his most of life there, and wrote with compassion about family, community, and the people he knew. For a brief period in 1925, he lived in New Orleans,  Louisiana. There, fellow writer Sherwood Anderson encouraged Faulkner to write fiction rather than poetry. So Faulkner created his _fictional_ region, Yoknapatawpha County which was the setting for most of his works. In the legendary county, southern white merchants, farmers, poor whites, and persecuted blacks appeared.

Faulkner spent most of his life writing brilliantly and constantly. With the publication in 1929 of his fourth novel, *The Sound and the Fury*, he got the readers' attention. Much of the novel was told from the viewpoint of a retarded boy. Faulkner earned two Pulitzer Prizes and the 1949 Nobel Prize for literature.

1. The word "fictional" in the passage is opposite in meaning to

    a. traditional

    b. brilliant

    c. real

    d. thrilling

2. When did Faulkner get the readers' attention?

    a. When he wrote about persecuted blacks

    b. When he began writing with Sherwood Anderson

    c. When he made Yoknapatawpha County in his works

    d. When his fourth novel was published

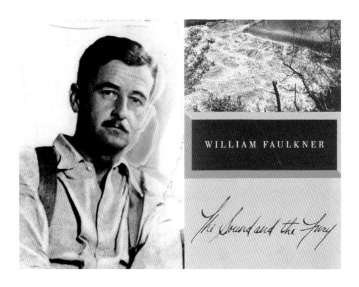

Actual Mini *TOEFL*

Read the following passage and answer questions.

George Orwell was the pen name for Eric Arthur Blair, an English novelist and social critic. He was born in Bengal, India, of the son of an English civil servant. He attended Eton University from 1917 to 1921 and served as the Indian Imperial Police in Burma from 1922 to 1927. He lived in poverty in England and Europe for a while after leaving Burma. He wrote his first book, *Down and Out in Paris and London*, which was a nonfiction of his poverty. His experience had more influenced on his novels and essays than anything else. His novels <u>*attacked*</u> social injustice and the miseries of the poor.

His novel *1984*, published in 1949, described totalitarian society in a frightening way. In another famous book, *Animal Farm*, he satirized communism. The book was a satire of the Russian Revolution of 1917 in particular. Because of this controversial subject matter, he had difficulty finding a publisher. British publishing house <u>*rejected*</u> his work. However, Orwell became famous as soon as the novel was eventually published in 1945. In the same month, the atomic bombs were dropped on Hiroshima and Nagasaki and drew <u>*attention*</u> of many readers and authors.

1. What does the passage mainly discuss?

    a. George Orwell's early life

    b. George Orwell's social work

    c. George Orwell's life and works

    d. George Orwell's influence on novelists

2. What was not true about this book, *Down and Out in Paris and London*?

    a. It was Orwell's first book.

    b. Orwell wrote about his poverty.

    c. It was about totalitarianism.

    d. Orwell wrote the book after leaving Burma.

3. What were Orwell's works the most influenced by?

    a. Orwell's experience

    b. Orwell's parents

    c. Orwell's study on communism

    d. English novels and essays

4. The word "attacked" in the passage is closest in meaning to

   a. expressed

   b. criticized

   c. praised

   d. found

5. What did *Animal Farm* mainly deal with?

   a. Miseries of poor people

   b. The Russian Recolution

   c. British civil servants

   d. Indian empire

6. The word "rejected" in the passage is opposite in meaning to

   a. understood

   b. declined

   c. delivered

   d. adopted

7. What is the word "attention" in the passage is closest in meaning to

   a. notice

   b. familiarity

   c. worry

   d. blame

08

Industry

8 Industry

I Write the word that "its" refers to

Pittsburgh once dominated world steel production and pushed the United States of America to world leadership as an industrial giant. Pittsburgh steel was used to build many  remarkable structures of the modern age: the Brooklyn Bridge, the Panama Canal locks, the Empire State Building, Rockefeller Centre, and the United Nations. During World War II, _its_ steel mills were working around the clock to make enough steel for America and its allies.

II Write the word or phrase that "They" refers to

Natural gas is one of the preferring fuels in many countries. It has the ecological advantage of causing less pollution. It is available in large amounts through vast reserves. It is relatively low in price in comparison to other alternative fuels. Its demand

increased gradually. Undoubtedly the natural gas industry was developed as a result of the strong investments made by gas transportation and distribution companies. _**They**_ invested in system improvements, client assistance and so on.

_____

III **Read the passage and answer questions.**

Detroit in Michigan is known as "Motor City." The city has been the heart of the American automobile industry. Its automobile industry provided a model for mass production. The use of the assembly lines and conveyor belts in manufacturing automobiles resulted in mass production and expense reduction. Factory workers work on different parts together quickly and relatively inexpensively. Each worker concentrates on doing the same job on each car. For example, someone might be responsible only for attaching rear view mirrors. This person would do the task so many times that he or she would become an expert at _it_ and be able to do it very quickly. Henry Ford produced the first car in this fashion. Now Ford is one of the leading companies in the world automobile market.

1. The word "it" in the passage refers to

   a. the use of the assembly line

   b. factory workers

   c. each worker

   d. attaching rear view mirrors

2. According to the passage, what does each worker do in the process of the mass production?

   a. He or she assembles each automobile.

   b. He or she does the same work all day.

   c. He or she attaches rear view mirrors.

   d. He or she produces a whole car.

IV Read the passage and answer questions.

The chemical industry in South Africa has had a long history, having been founded late in the nineteenth century. As South Africa has no oil reserves and little natural gas, its chemical industry has primarily developed based on the liquefaction of coal. After refining the first oil from a coal plant at Sasolburg, the petrochemical industry was established.

The chemical industry focused on the local market during the apartheid years. _**It**_ depended on small-scale plants which managed to meet the local demand and which tended to be uneconomical. These locally processed goods have generally been less competitive in export market. Now that South Africa is once fully part of the global community, South African chemical companies are focusing on the need to be internationally competitive. The industry is reshaping itself accordingly.

1. What does the word "It" in the passage refers to?

    a. The chemical industry

    b. Local market

    c. Apartheid

    d. South Africa

2. What was the resource for the early chemical industry of South Africa?

    a. Oil

    b. Natural gas

    c. Coal

    d. Gold

V Read the passage and answer questions.

The timber industry continued to grow in decades to keep up the pace with the demand for wood products. Development of  equipment such as the log truck, and the chainsaw increased the efficiency of the industry, lowered **_its_** costs, and increased production quickly. The timber industry, like other industries, brought fortune to many people.

From 1945 to 1970, the timber harvest increased faster than the growth of the national economy. This increase was important for the expansion of softwood and plywood production. By the mid-twentieth century, large companies had integrated their operations. Logging, sawing, and pulping typically undertaken by single company were located at the same site, which was easy to transfer pulpwood chips. With new investments, the timber industry has had a great influence on the economy.

1. The word "its" in the passage refers to

    a. the equipment

    b. the log truck

    c. the timber industry

    d. the national economy

2. What caused the production of timber to increase?

    a. The increase in population

    b. The development of equipment

    c. The investments on the timber industry

    d. The integration of companies

Actual Mini *TOEFL*

Read the following passage and answer questions.

By the time the textile industry in England had reached its peak, Samuel Slater emigrated secretly to America in 1789. Though it was against British law for a textile worker to leave the country, *he* fled to seek his fortune in America.

While others with experience of textile manufacturing had emigrated before him, Slater was the first man who knew how to build textile machines, as well as how to operate them.

Slater built the first American water powered textile mill in Pawtucket in 1793. Considered the father of the United States textile industry, he eventually built several successful cotton mills in New England and *established* the town of Slatersville. The factories offered jobs to labors desperate for work. Entire families labored together in the textile mills. *They* often lived in the company owned housing near the mills, shopped at the company stores, and attended company schools and churches.

Before the Civil War, textile manufacturing was the most important industry in America and there were *rapid* advances in mill technology. The cotton industry drew thousands of immigrants from around the world.

1. What is the best title for the passage?

    a. The rapid development of the American Industry

    b. Samuel Slater's contribution to the world

    c. Laborers looking for works

    d. The initiator of the American textile industry

2. What does the word "he" in the passage refers to

    a. England

    b. Samuel Slater

    c. British law

    d. a textile worker

3. Why did Samuel Slater move to America secretly?

    a. He, as a textile worker, was prohibited to leave his country.

    b. He lost his fortune in Britain.

    c. He was the first person who knew how to build textile machines.

    d. He was considered to be the best textile worker.

4. The word "established" in the passage is closest in meaning to

    a. discovered

    b. invented

    c. organized

    d. recovered

5. The word "They" in the passage refers to

    a. New England

    b. The factories

    c. Entire families

    d. The textile mills

6. What was Slater's textile mill run by?

    a. By horses

    b. By water

    c. By cotton

    d. By computer

7. All of the following are true about Samuel Slater except

    a. He was a first emigrated textile worker.

    b. He set up textile mills in America.

    c. He facilitated the American cotton industry.

    d. He knew how to build textile machines.

8. The word "rapid" in the passage is opposite in meaning to

    a. outstanding

    b. admirable

    c. permanent

    d. slow

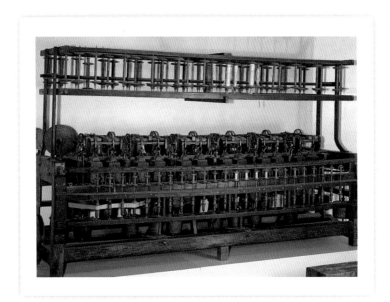

09

Archeology

9 Archeology

I Arrange the following sentences in order.

a. They found that it was hand painted glass of the 14th century.

b. Rabbits were digging on farmland to make their own home.

c. Archeologist races to the farmland to investigate the glass.

d. They also learned that it should be in safekeeping not to be exposed to the air.

e. In the course of digging, they unearthed the remains of a rare glass window.

_____

Ⅱ Choose and write the sentence that comes in each blank.

A city of Taino Indians has been found recently on the island of Hispania. Archeologists have discovered the Taino city in the jungle of the Dominican Republic. The city has three plazas.

_____

The most important find so far is a well that is 35 meters deep.

_____

Scuba divers have found carved wooden axes, baskets, and pottery.

_____

a. This natural well contained many Taino artifacts.

b. They were probably used for ceremonies and a Taino game similar to soccer.

c. The Indians probably dropped the items into the water as religious offerings.

III **Read the passage and answer questions.**

Archeology is the scientific study of people of the past. The purpose of archeology is to understand how humans in the past lived in their environment and preserve this history for present and

future learning. *(A)* Archeologists usually work in teams with other archeologists or archeology students. *(B)* They investigate clues to learn how humans in the past lived. *(C)* They work at a dig site to gather data, and then analyze the data in a lab. *(D)* They eventually write reports on their findings.

The type of work that archeologists do require a great deal of patience and perseverance. According to where the dig sites are located, the conditions in which they work may be extremely bad. It is steaming hot, freezing cold, or lack of water. Most archeologists are willing to tolerate these conditions because they know that their work can lead to new theories about past humans and the way they lived.

1. The following sentence can be added to the passage.

> Most of them belong to a university or a museum.

   Where would it best fit in the passage?

2. According to the passage, where do archeologists work to gather data?
   a. In a lab
   b. At a museum
   c. In a desert
   d. At a dig site

IV Read the passage and answer questions.

    GIS is a convenient tool for handling and organizing data. GIS stands for Geographic Information System. GIS technology has been used in finding water resources, analyzing climate and discovering dig sites for archeologists. It can be widely used for scientific investigations, resource management, and development planning.

    GIS is a computer system capable of collecting, storing, handling, and displaying geographically reference information. *(A)* The computers also can perform complex analyses with these data. *(B)* The condition of the earth's surface, atmosphere and subsurface can be examined by feeding satellite data into a GIS. *(C)* Maps can be built with various information gathered by GIS. *(D)* GIS technology gives researchers the ability to examine the process of the earth over days, months and years.

1. The following sentence can be added to the passage.

> The computers capture and file the data.

Where would it best fit in the passage?

2. Which of the following is not GIS used for?

   a. Scientific investigation

   b. Development planning

   c. Resource creation

   d. Discovery of dig site

V Read the passage and answer questions.

(A) It is a archeologists' great interest as well as their mission to find archeological sites. *(B)* First of all, they have to find what environmental factors humans have always needed in order to stay alive. *(C)* The factors include easy access to water, the location on a trade route, and the geographical location that protects people from natural disasters. *(D)* With the information in mind, archeologists can study maps to locate likely places where prehistoric people may have lived.

In addition to this, archeologists often find sites with the help of construction companies. They open land to build houses, schools, and other structures and they sometimes uncover artifacts. Construction crews are required to report their discoveries of artifacts and relics to a local archeologist. In this way, archeologists cooperate with construction crews to investigate the potential sites.

1. The following sentence can be added to the passage.

> So, they have studied ways to find the sites.

   Where would it best fit in the passage?

2. What will construction crews do if they find artifacts?

   a. They will stop construction.

   b. They will cover the artifacts.

   c. They will contact archeologists.

   d. They will investigate the artifacts.

Actual Mini *TOEFL*

Read the following passage and answer questions.

It was in 79 A. D. when Mt. Vesuvius suddenly erupted and the entire city of Pompeii was covered with ashes. Volcanic matter continued to cover the city  for three days. Structures and people were encased in the ash. Two thousand people died. The town remained buried for almost two thousand years.

Until recently, archeologists spent most of their time uncovering the city. At the beginning of the Pompeii *excavation*, archeologists tried to find art objects. As time went by, *they* found wide areas, buried towns, destructed buildings, and ruined houses. Many famous scholars studied the remains of Pompeii. They *classified* the uncovered architecture and artifacts.

(A) The Romans built high footpaths on each side of the street. *(B)* Millstones and ovens for baking bread were used. *(C)* The Romans could do the baths and have a quick lunch at one of many cafes. *(D)*

At present, the archeologists try to reconstruct the city's social and cultural life. In the hands of new generation of researchers, ancient Pompeii is coming to life again.

1. What is the main topic of the passage?

    a. The work of archeologists

    b. The tragedy of Pompeii

    c. Archeological study of Pompeii

    d. A study on the Roman society and culture

2. How long did Pompeii stay buried after the eruption of Vesuvius?

    a. For about two thousand years

    b. For about two hundred years

    c. For about one thousand years

    d. For about one hundred years

3. The word "excavation" in the passage is closest in meaning to

    a. rescue

    b. search

    c. dig

    d. Eruption

4. The word "they" in the passage refers to

    a. art object

    b. volcanic matter

    c. archeologists

    d. the Romans

5. The word "classified" in the passage is closest in meaning to

    a. confined

    b. assorted

    c. analyzed

    d. compared

6. All of the following were the ways the Romans lived around 79 A.D. except

    a. They enjoyed taking a bath.

    b. They ate bread.

    c. They spent item at cafes.

    d. They rode wagons.

7. The following sentence can be added to the passage.

> By studying the remains of Pompeii, archeologists have learned a lot about the way the Romans lived.

Where would it best fit in the passage?

8. **Which of the following describes the recent work of Archeologists for Pompeii?**

    a. They examined art objects.

    b. They reconstructed the city's social life.

    c. They classify the uncovered artifacts.

    d. They build the high footpaths on the street.

10

Musicians

10 Musicians

I Arrange the following sentences in order.

1. The first performance of *American Festival Overture* was conducted in 1939.

2. In 1962, Schumann became president of Lincoln Center for the Performing Arts in New York.

3. He composed his famous cantata, *A Free Song* in 1942.

4. Born in New York on August 4, 1910, William Schumann began composing while in high school.

5. The National Medal of Arts was awarded to Schumann in 1987.

Ⅱ Choose and write the sentence that comes in each blank.

Jose Moncayo was born in Mexico.

_____

_____. He entered Mexico City

Conservatory, where he continued his piano studies and

composition. His first professional job was a percussionist with

the Mexican State Symphony Orchestra. _____

_____. Moncayo tried to write music that

reflected the nationalistic spirit of Mexico.

_____.

a. Later, he conducted the National Symphony Orchestra from
   1949 to 1954.

b. He used melodies, rhythms, and harmonies from the folk music
   of Mexico.

c. He learned piano as a boy.

III Read the passage and answer questions.

Leonard Bernstein was a pioneer in the field of music in America. He was the first American-born composer and conductor to receive worldwide recognition.

(A) Bernstein began playing the piano when he was ten years old. *(B)* He graduated from Harvard, and then from the Curtis Institute of Music, where he studied piano, conducting, and composition. *(C)* When he was an assistant conductor of the New York Philharmonic, he had a special chance to take the place of the regular conductor one evening. *(D)* He was the regular conductor of the New York Philharmonic from 1958 through 1969. Throughout his career, he conducted many concerts for young students.

Bernstein traveled the world as a conductor and encouraged appreciation of the music of American composers. Bernstein also composed classical music, Broadway music, and jazz.

1. The following sentence can be added to the passage.

> He did such an outstanding job
> that many orchestras wanted to hire him.

   Where would it best fit in the passage?

2. Which of the following is true about Bernstein?

   a. He spent his life only conducting.

   b. He was recognized only in America.

   c. He conducted a lot of concerts for young people.

   d. He began composing at the age of ten.

IV **Read the passage and answer questions.**

Igor Stravinsky was a Russian composer who created great change in his music as well as in his life. (A) The music for the ballet *The Fire Bird* was his strikingly original composition and made him famous as a composer. (B) He composed more ballet music including  *Petrushka* and *the Rite of Spring*. (C) In addition, when the ballet was first played in public, it caused a riot. (D) The audience argued about the music and made so much noise that the sound of music was drowned out. His music influenced many other modern composers, especially in the United States and France.

He later became an American citizen. He continued to write music, but it was not very popular. He created music that was different from what had been heard before. He was a talented and inventive composer in changing styles. He may be seen as the musical counterpart of the painter Picasso.

1. The following sentence can be added to the passage.

> In *the Rite of Spring*, Stravinsky used
> irregular and primitive rhythms.

   Where would it best fit in the passage?

2. Which of the following word best describe Stravinsky's music?

   a. Inventive

   b. Classical

   c. Romantic

   d. Simple

V **Read the passage and answer questions.**

(A) Duke Ellington was one of the founding members of jazz music. (B) When he was only four years old, he said that a piano tune he was listening was very pretty. (C) At the age of seven, he started playing the piano himself, and by the time he was 15, he was composing. (D) In his teens, his music was influenced by ragtime pianists.

In 1917, Duke began playing music professionally in Washington. When he was 20, he and his friends formed a band. Playing of his band was often broadcasted live on the radio from the Cotton Club, which made Ellington famous. The band made the change from hot jazz to swing music. In the 1960s, Duke wrote several religious pieces and collaborated with various musicians. A pianist, band leader, and composer, Ellington and his band continued to attract outstanding musicians even after his death.

1. The following sentence can be added to the passage.

> At an early age, he loved music.

   Where would it best fit in the passage?

2. All of the following are related with Ellington except

   a. He played jazz music.

   b. He worked with the band.

   c. Playings of his band were broadcast on the radio.

   d. He sang for his band.

Actual Mini *TOEFL*

Read the following passage and answer questions.

Zoltan Kodaly was a Hungarian composer and educator who lived during the 19th and 20th centuries. His music was influenced the most by Hungarian folk music.  He collected, analyzed, edited and *organized* Hungarian folk songs, including field recording to preserve Hungarian culture.

Kodaly inspired a revolution in teaching of music in Hungary. (A) He believed that music belonged to everyone and to achieve a higher level of musical understanding, music training had to be developed within school systems. (B) He advocated a love of music supported by knowledge about music. (C) He established new *principles* for music education for Hungarians. (D) Kodaly's method of teaching music was based on their own folk music. *This* formed the starting point for musical learning which eventually lead to an understanding of music of all styles, genres, and cultures.

He received many awards and honors and continued his efforts to improve Hungarian music education. His many essays on music education and the use of the folk song in teaching children have influenced teachers and music curriculum all over the world.

1. What is the main idea of the passage?

   a. Zoltan Kodaly spent most of his time conducting Hungarian music.

   b. Zoltan Kodaly contributed to Hungarian music education.

   c. Zoltan Kodaly made the most famous Hungarian music.

   d. Zoltan Kodaly left many essays and methods on folk music.

2. The word "organized" in the passage is closest in meaning to

   a. announced

   b. gathered

   c. systemized

   d. preferred

3. The following sentence can be added to the passage.

> These principles have been known as the
> "Kodaly Method" of music education.

Where would it best fit in the passage?

4. Which of the following is not true about Zoltan Kodaly?

a. He was a composer in the 19th century.

b. He was influenced by European music.

c. He wrote many essays on music education.

d. He received many awards and honors.

5. What did Zoltan Kodaly think most people should do to love music?

a. They should collect folk songs.

b. They should graduate from a music college.

c. They should know about music.

d. They should compose their own music.

6. The word "principles" in the passage is closest in meaning to

   a. principals

   b. rules

   c. tools

   d. projects

7. The word "This" in the passage refers to

   a. Knowledge about music

   b. A love of music

   c. Music education

   d. Kodaly's method of teaching music

8. What was not Kodaly's concept of music education?

   a. Students must understand all genres of music.

   b. Music belongs to everyone.

   c. Music education must be based on folk music.

   d. Musical training must be done within school systems.

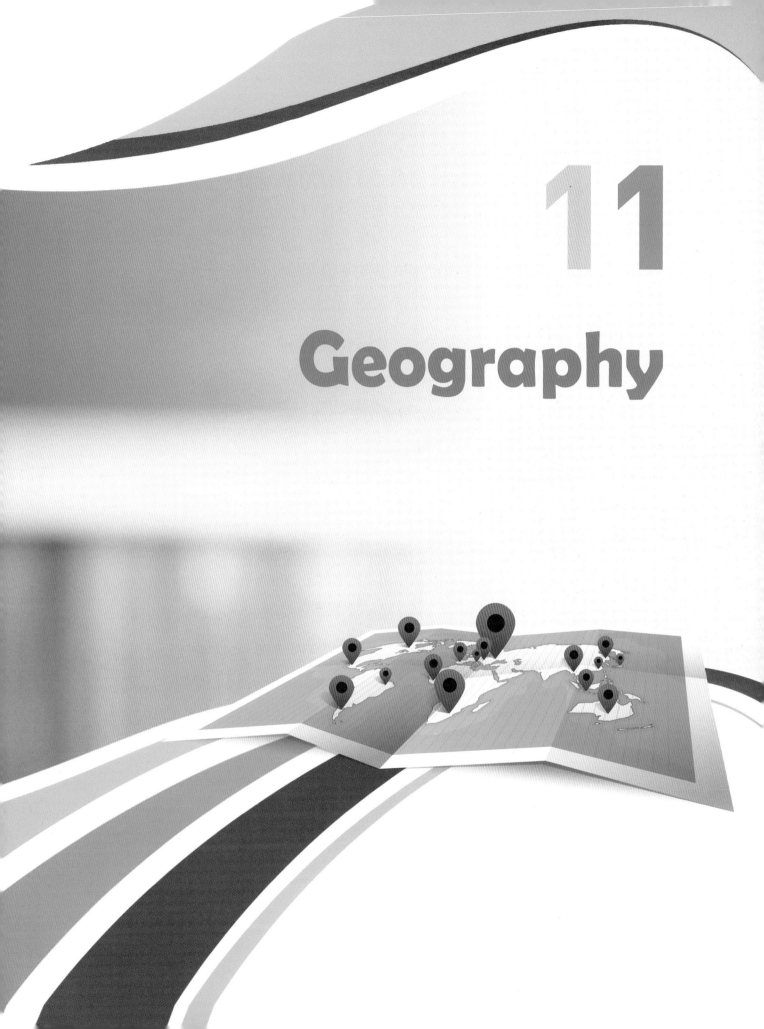

11 Geography

(11) Geography

I **Write the word that is closest in meaning to chief.**

Singapore consists of the island of Singapore and about 60 small islands at the southern tip of the Malay Peninsula. The capital is Singapore City that is a _chief_ port.

Singapore has a tropical rainforest climate with high temperature and rainfall all the year. Over 75% of the population is Chinese. Its religions are Buddhism, Islam, Hinduism, Confucianism, and Christianity. Four languages including English are spoken and it has the high literacy rate. Commerce is the chief source of income. Singapore reexports rubber, petroleum, timber, and textiles that it imports. And it imports most of its food requirements.

_____

II Write the word that is **OPPOSITE** in meaning to includes.

The earth is covered with water and land. Water _included_ oceans, lakes, and rivers. Oceans are the largest bodies of water. The Pacific Ocean is the largest ocean on the earth. A lake is a body of water surrounded with land. A river flows across the land.

The Nile is the longest river in the world. Land on the earth is divided into flat land, hills, and mountains. Flat land is a called plain. A hill is land that is higher than the land around it. Mountains are the highest kind of land. Mt. Everest is the highest mountain on the earth.

_____

😊 Reading Passage 1

Read the passage and answer questions.

When a map is drawn, it is not possible to show things in real size. Maps show things smaller by making use of a scale. Every map has its scale clearly printed on the front. Because maps are used by a lot of people, the scale has to be very *accurate*.

The scale tells how much smaller the area on the map is shown when compared to the same area in the real world. It is usually written like this, "1:25,000." This means that things in real size are 25,000 times as large as those on the map.

Large-scale maps are better for showing things in detail because they only cover a small area of land. Small-scale maps are better for travelling by car or on foot because they cover large areas of land. The larger is the scale of a map, the smaller area can be seen on the map.

1. The word "accurate" in the passage is closest in meaning to

   a. wrong

   b. exact

   c. small

   d. wild

2. How long in the real world is a 5-centimeter long river on a map
   in the scale of 1:50,000?

   a. 2,500 km

   b. 250m

   c. 25km

   d. 2,500 m

Reading Passage 2

Read the passage and answer questions.

Mongolia is a large country in Northern Asia and it is bordered by Russia on the north and China on the south. The Gobi Desert covers the southern part of the land. The central and the

northern parts of Mongolia located on the Siberian steppe which is dry and flat grassland.

Mongolia's winter is harsh and lasts from October to April. Summer days are hot and accompanied by dust storms. In some areas, there is not enough natural fresh water. Traditionally, Mongolians lead a nomadic way of life. Nomadic life means moving from place to place to find the grass for the animals they raise, including cattle, sheep, goats, horses, and camels. Animal husbandry is the mainstay of the Mongolian economy. The country produces about one third of the world's cashmere, wool from sheep. Agriculture is limited because only 18% of the land is arable. Recently, rapid urbanization and industrial growth have had negative effects on the environment.

1. The word "natural" in the passage is OPPOSITE in meaning to

    a. normal

    b. clean

    c. real

    d. artificial

2. All of the following are true about Mongolia EXCEPT

    a. Its mainstay is agriculture.

    b. It produces quite a large amount of cashmere.

    c. It became urbanized rapidly.

    d. It has very cold weather in winter.

Reading Passage 3

Read the passage and answer questions.

Millions of years ago the earth's surface was covered with much more ice than it is today. The massive sheets of ice moved slowly across the landscape. As the ice sheets moved, they carved valley or **_deposited_** materials. The moving ice sheets are called glaciers.

According to how big and powerful a glacier is, it can change a shape of a valley as it moves along. Before the glacier arrives, the valley may have been much narrower and shallower. The force of ice moving through the valley has made the valley floor wider and its sides steeper. The valley that has changed to a U-shape is sometimes called a glacier trough.

Hanging valleys are formed by smaller glaciers which do not have the power to erode the landscape.

Snowdonia is the mountainous area of North Wales that has been shaped by glaciers. Many of the features associated with glaciers can be found there.

1. What is the word "deposited" in the passage closest in meaning to

   a. sliced

   b. floated

   c. settled

   d. removed

2. What has shaped the feature of Snowdonia?

   a. Wind

   b. Glaciers

   c. Snow

   d. Storms

Actual Mini TOEFL

Read the passage and answer questions.

Switzerland is a tiny country located in central Europe. About two thirds of country is covered with forest, lakes, and mountains. It is surrounded all sides by land. Two mountain ranges, the Jura and the Alps, separate the country from their neighbors. The mountains have also helped keep Switzerland out of wars. When Switzerland was founded in 1291, it had three cantons. Gradually 20 cantons were added to the country. Switzerland **_declared_** its neutrality in 1812. Since it remains forever neutral, all the headquarters of international organization are located in Switzerland.

This country has four official languages. In western Switzerland most people speak French. To the north, most people speak German. In the southeast there are Italian-speaking Swiss. All of these languages can be heard in Bern, Switzerland's capital.

The most important part of its economy is service including banking, assurance, and tourism. Since Switzerland has no mineral resources, it must import, process, and resell them as **_products._** Handmade clocks, tools, and furniture are its famous products. The country is also **_famous_** for its dairy products. Medicines, dyes, and textiles are important exports.

1. Which of the following best describes the geographical characteristic of Switzerland?

   a. It is landlocked.

   b. It is an island.

   c. It is a peninsula.

   d. It is a desert.

2. The word "declare" in the passage is closest in meaning to

   a. elected

   b. proclaimed

   c. decided

   d. argued

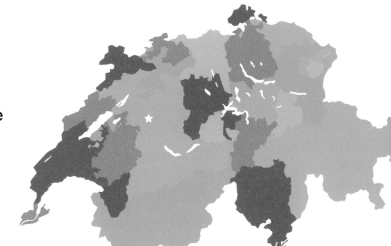

3. Why do international organization locate their headquarters in Switzerland?

   a. Because it is the most beautiful country.

   b. Because it supplies cheap building.

   c. Because it is covered with mountains.

   d. Because it is a permanent neutral country.

4. **All of the following describe the Swiss EXCEPT**

   a. They have four official languages.

   b. Many of them work in the service industry.

   c. They export mineral resources.

   d. They live in a small country.

5. **What is the main topic of paragraph 3?**

   a. The languages of Switzerland

   b. The history of Switzerland

   c. The industry of Switzerland

   d. The future of Switzerland

6. The word "products" in the passage is closest in meaning to

   a. crops

   b. standards

   c. lists

   d. goods

7. The word "famous" in the passage is OPPOSITE in meaning to

   a. well-known

   b. unknown

   c. valuable

   d. poor

12

International Relationships

12 International Relationships

I Choose the fact that can be inferred from the passage.

The Middle East is located at the junction of three continents-Europe, Asia, and Africa. The Middle East has historically been a crossroad for conquerors, trade, and ideas as well as a transition zone for political and cultural interation.

This area is also the birthplace of the world's religions such as Judaism, Christianity, and Islam. Since the start of 20th century, the Middle East has been the center of world affairs because of its strategic location and its vast petroleum reserves.

a. There are no Muslim people in Middle East.

b. The Middle East has been an important place for trade.

c. The Middle East was formed in the 20th century.

Read the passage and draw O if the following statements can be inferred and draw X if they cannot.

The Asia-Pacific Economic Cooperation(APEC) is a group of countries that meet to discuss the economic growth, cooperation, trade, and

Asia-Pacific Economic Cooperation

investment in the Asia-Pacific region.

The special characteristic about this group is that it does not compel its members to make any promises. Everything that the member countries agree on is made on a voluntarily basis. APEC now has 21 members. Since 1989, it has reduced tariffs and increased trade across the Asia-Pacific region.

a. More members are joined APEC. ___

b. APEC has accomplished much since 1989. ___

c. Members of APEC respect the opinion of each member.

d. The United States is not a member of APEC.

👀 Reading Passage 1

Read the following passage and answer questions.

The United Nations is looked up to by many people as the peacekeeper of the world. The idea for the organization was first discussed two years before World War II ended. Countries around the world

wanted to prevent another world war. After 51 countries decided on the purpose of the organization, its membership, and the arrangements to maintain international peace, they signed to approve its establishment. The UN was formally established on October 24, 1945. It now has 191 member countries out of 192 independent states worldwide.

Countries that joined the UN must accept the conditions including developing friendly relations with countries, solving international problems, and promoting respect for human rights. Although the UN helps resolve international conflicts, it is not a world government and it does not make laws.

1. It can be inferred from the passage that

    a. the UN has the power to make international rules.

    b. the UN was established before world war II ended.

    c. the UN was the idea of the United States.

    d. almost all independent nations are members of the UN.

2. What was the original intent of the countries that wanted to form
    the United Nations?

    a. They wanted to defeat enemy countries in World War II.

    b. They wanted to keep a world war from happening again.

    c. They wanted to make an international law-making body.

    d. They wanted to form a world government.

Reading Passage 2

Read the following passage and answer questions.

The United Nations High Commissioner for Refugees(UNHCR) plays an important role in helping refugees around the world. Refugees are people who have been forced to leave their countries. There are many reasons why people would have no choice but to leave. Sometimes, people leave because a war breaks out in their nations. Another reason is that the country's government treats them badly to make them obey a bad leader. The other reason is that the religious leaders hurt the people. When a person leaves his country, he becomes stateless. Therefore, it is easy for other countries to do something wrong to him. This is why the UNHCR comes in.

The UNHCR protects refugees and helps them find a new home or return to their countries. Until 2004, the UNHCR has helped more than 50 million refugees around the world since 1950.

1. Which of the following can be inferred from the passage?

    a. The UNHCR prevents countries from doing wrong to refugees.

    b. The UNHCR cannot help the old refugees.

    c. Refugees never return to their countries.

    d. Refugees can choose the country they want to go to.

2. What is not a reason why a person leaves his country?

    a. Bad religious leader

    b. War

    c. Joblessness

    d. Bad government

Reading Passage 3

Read the following passage and answer questions.

The G7 is a union of the major industrial democracies of the world. Its main purpose is to have the financial ministers of each member country

meet each year to discuss world economic and political issues. Members of the first meeting included six countries, the United Kingdom, France, Germany, Italy, Japan, and the United States. In 1976, the members became 7 by Canada's joining the group. Finally, it became G8 in 1998 with the acceptance of Russia as a full member.

The G7/8 discusses world economy, international trade, and relations with developing countries, but it has included important subjects in its annual meeting. Some subjects that have been talked about are energy and environment, terrorism, crime and drugs, human rights, and arms control. Arms control is a limitation in the size and weapons of the armed forces.

1. It can be inferred from the passage that

   a. the G7 has no member countries from Asia.

   b. the G7 has been growing.

   c. only economic and political issues are discussed.

   d. the G7 had the 7 members in 1998.

2. Which of the following has not been discussed at G7/8 meetings?

   a. Problems with terrorism

   b. Environmental pollution

   c. Space research

   d. Sources of Energy

Actual Mini *TOEFL*

Read the passage and answer questions.

"Tunza" is the name given by the United Nations Environment Program(UNEP) to attract young people around the world. Tunza is a word from the Kiswahili language that is used in Eastern Africa and it means "to treat with care and affection." By holding Tunza International Youth Conference, the UNEP is giving young people of the ages 15 to 24 the opportunity to treat the environment with care and ***affection***. It encourages ***them*** to promote the environmental protection and sustainable development. Sustainable development is economic development without using up natural resources and without polluting the environment.

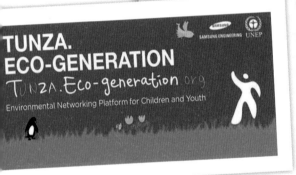

___(A) The last Tunza International Youth Conference was held in Dubna, Russia in August 2003. ___(B) One hundred fifty young people attended the conference. ___(C) The theme for 2003 was "A Time for Action." On the last day of the conference, the participants outlined ten things that they would do when they returned to their countries. ___(D) These included changing their lifestyle to show greater ***awareness*** of the environment, organizing gathering to support environmental activities, and working with school officials to promote environmental education.

1. What is the main topic of the passage?

    a. The Tunza International Youth Conference

    b. A Time for Action

    c. The United Nations Environment Program

    d. Environmental Protection and Sustainable Development

2. It can be inferred from the passage that

    a. all the youth want to know what is happening to the environment.

    b. the role of young people in environmental issues

    c. the Tunza conference makes young people learn the value of environment.

    d. the first Tunza Conference was held in 2003.

3. Where does the word "Tunza" come from?

    a. France

    b. Dubna

    c. The United States

    d. Africa

4. The word "affection" in the passage is closest in meaning to

    a. praise

    b. similarity

    c. love

    d. peace

5. The word "them" in the passage refers to

    a. opportunities

    b. young people

    c. the United Nations

    d. natural resources

6. The word "awareness" in the passage is opposite in meaning to

    a. ignorance

    b. respect

    c. knowledge

    d. acceptance

7. The following sentence can be added to the passage.

> These young people have shown an interest
> in the environment by engaging in
> environmental activities in their own countries.

8. Which of the following is not an action the Tunza Conference participants will do when they return to their countries?

a. Having environmental issues taught in school

b. Running everyday along the river

c. Cleaning the park near their houses

d. Forming groups to take part in environmental services

13

Language

12 Language

I Write the word that they refer to.

Not using literal or phonetic language, animal communication can take place using visual and auditory methods.

Honeybees communicate the location of food source by dancing when _**they**_ return to the hive. Features of dance inform other bees about the direction and the distance of the food source. Male frog calls are loud enough to attract females but do not inform predators of their location. Bats can use echolocation as a form of communication as well as a hunting tool.

_____

II Write the word or phrase that they refer to.

All human talks, but pets or house plants don't talk however well **_they_** are taught and trained. Therefore, heredity is involved in language.

A child growing up in Korea speaks Korean whereas the same child growing up in Ontario would speak English. That shows environment is also involved in language. Thus, there is no question about both heredity and environment being involved in language.

_____

☺ **Reading Passage 1**

Read the passage and answer question.

Sign language is a language spoken with hands. It is a language for people who can't talk or hear. When a person can't hear or has severe hearing problems, he is called deaf. Some people are born deaf. Others become deaf because of 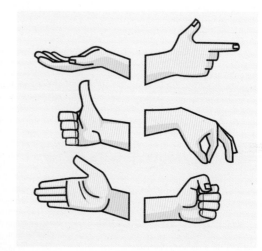 an illness, an accident, or just from getting older. When a person is unable to speak, he is called mute.

Sign language was invented so that deaf or mute people can communicate with others. They are the same as hearing people because they can go to school, get jobs, see movies, get married, and have families. They just use sign language and interpreters to help *them.*

In American Sign Language speakers leave out words like and, were, was, them, and they. There is another kind of sign language called English Sign Language. In English Sign Language no words are left out.

1. The word "them" in the passage refers to

    a. deaf or mute people

    b. hearing people

    c. some families

    d. interpreters

2. According to the passage, which of the following is not the cause of being deaf?

    a. Illness

    b. Accidents

    c. Neighbors

    d. Old age

👁 **Reading Passage 2**

Read the following passage and answer questions.

From ancient times, many different races spoke their own language, but not all the races had an alphabet. Some people borrowed other languages to write their spoken language, which gave them trouble learning how to write it. There were some representative languages which were based on an alphabet created from ancient times.

Chinese writing had more than 50,000 characters, but using only 5,000 of the most common characters they could read letters or books. _Ancient Egyptian alphabets were written in rows or columns. The rows could be written left to write or right to left. The columns could be written top to bottom. They_ were used for many religious texts. Roman Numerals were symbols that stand for numbers. All Roman numerals were written using some different symbols. They were written from the left side to the right side, using the rule of addition in most cases.

1. Look at the word "They" in the passage. Write the word that it refers to.

   _____

2. What happened to the people who were using a different alphabet from their spoken language?

   a. They forgot how to speak their language.

   b. They had great difficulty learning how to write.

   c. They changed their language.

   d. They used symbols for common words.

Reading Passage 3

Read the following passage and answer questions.

Today's English is quite different from that of Shakespearian times around the 17th century. As a language changes, using different styles of speaking over the

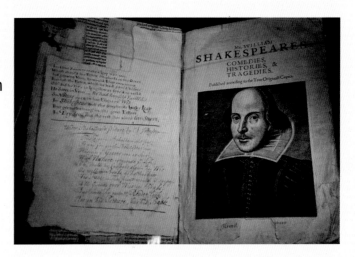

ages, the language of Shakespearian times has changed.

Many of today's words were used in a different way or never used in Shakespearian's time. Shakespearian speakers said "thou" and "ye" instead of "you." **_They_** said "bootless boil-brained clack-dish as an insult, instead of "mindless idiot." They did not use words like "primitive."

On the contrary, some other Shakespearian words are not understandable or sound strange to today's common speakers. "Tickle-brain, "a kind of strong alcoholic drink, is not used today. In a common conversation, they said "Nephew, ye wish for drink?" Today's common speakers will say, "Hey, you want a drink?"

1. What does the word "They" in the passage refers to.

    a. Today's words

    b. Today's people

    c. Shakespearian words

    d. Shakespearian speakers

2. Which of the following word was not used in Shakespearian times?

    a. Thou

    b. Primitive

    c. Tickle-brain

    d. Nephew

Actual Mini *TOEFL*

Read the following passage and answer questions.

Language is regarded as a clear vehicle for communicating idea. Even when it is used literally, however, misunderstandings arise and meanings shift. Moreover, figurative language is often used. Figurative language is words and phrases that mean something other than **_their_** usual meaning. Figurative language includes simile, a metaphor, and personification.

A simile is a comparison of two **_unlike_** things that uses the words "like" or "as." A metaphor is a direct comparison between two unlike things that does not use the word "like" or "as." Personification is a figure of speech in which an animal, object, or idea is given human **_qualities_** or characteristics.

Authors use figurative language to make their writing vivid so that readers can imagine people, objects, and events more clearly. Figurative language is used in everyday speech as well as in poetry and fiction. Most people do not realize that much of their language consists of figures for effect and for emphasis. Understanding how **_it_** works helps people interpret what other people are really saying, and what they are trying to say.

1. What is the main idea of paragraph 3?

    a. Figurative language is a way to express thoughts and emotions.

    b. Figurative language is only used in literature.

    c. Figurative language causes misunderstandings between authors and readers.

    d. Figurative language is often -used language by common people as well as authors.

2. The word "their" in the passage refers to

    a. communicating idea

    b. misunderstandings

    c. figurative languages

    d. words and phrases

3. Which of the following sentences in an example of a simile?

    a. Time is gold.

    b. Time flows like a river.

    c. Time crawls, walks, runs, and flies later.

    d. Time is precious.

4. The word "unlike" in the passage is opposite in meaning to

    a. similar

    b. different

    c. various

    d. opposite

5. All of the following describe figurative language except

    a. It is a type of a literature.

    b. It is used in common conversation.

    c. Personification is a type of figurative language.

    d. It makes a poem vivid and clear.

6. According to the passage, why do people use figurative language in everyday speech?

    a. To be humorous

    b. To emphasize

    c. To focus on their ideas

    d. To make others understand clearly

7. The word "qualities" in the passage is closest in meaning to

    a. merits

    b. styles

    c. features

    d. belongings

8. Look at the word "it" in the passage. What does it refer to?

_____

14

Types of Art

14 Types of Art

I Write the word or phrase that it refers to.

A style is the way in which something is expressed or performed. A style's name usually has a word that helps explain the picture of *it*. For instance, impressionism could  have something to do with impression when artists make a painting. Cubism probably has something to do with cubes or shapes. Naturalism deals with objects in a natural way. Pop art is related to themes and techniques from mass culture.

_____

II **Write the word or phrase that its refers to.**

The portrait was a main subject in colonial and federal American art, because settlers sought to establish their identities in a new world. Immigrants to New World attempted to

bring Old World civilization to their wild surroundings.

When the Revolutionary War ended in 1783, artists sought to create a distinctive environment from the ideals of liberty. After the new nation achieved *__its__* independence, landscapes and scenes of nature began to express its unique qualities and characteristics.

_____

👀 **Reading Passage 1**

Read the passage and answer question.

Surrealism is a style in art history in which artists create dreamlike paintings filled with mysterious objects or familiar objects that have been changed in weird ways. Objects in paintings are realistically 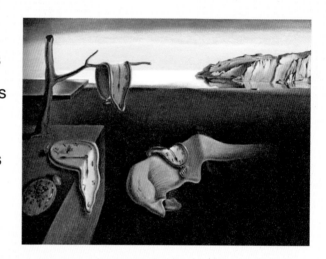 painted but they are rearranged or their shape is altered, which make them dreamlike.

In Salvador Dali's painting *The Persistence of Memory*, there are melting clocks and a clock with ants coming out of _it_. The clocks look real, but they are melting.

Rene Magritte's painting *Not to be Reproduced* is an example of a painting with mysterious objects. There are two reflections in a mirror: a person and a book. The book's reflection is correct, but the person's reflection is of the back of his head instead of his face. Magritte's painting *Son of Man* is another example of a surrealist painting with a man fixed with an apple on his face.

1. What does "it" in the passage refers to?

_____

2. Which of the following is not an example of surrealistic features?

   a. Clocks are melting.

   b. Books are reflected in a mirror.

   c. The reflection of a face is the back of the head.

   d. An apple is fixed on a man's face.

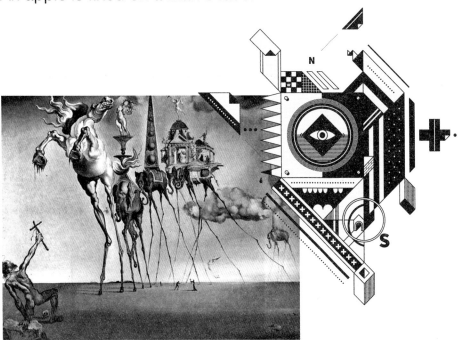

👀 Reading Passage 2

Read the following passage and answer questions.

In the painting of abstract art, there is not an accurate representation of a form or an object. Abstract artists felt that paintings did not have to show only things that were recognizable. Abstract artists did not try show people, animals, or places exactly as **they** appeared in the real world.

They mainly used colour and shape in their paintings to express their emotion. Some abstract art is also called non-objective art. There are no specific objects.

There are three forms of abstract styles that really stand out: cubism, neoplasticism, and abstract expressionism. There are many abstract artists who painted in these styles. For example, the most famous cubist was Pablo Picasso. One of the best examples of neoplasticism is Piet Mondrian. Mark Rothko and Jackson Pollock are famous artists of abstract expressionism.

1. The word "they" in the passage refers to

   a. abstract artists

   b. abstract paintings

   c. people, animals, or places

   d. emotions

2. What did abstract artists use to express emotions in their paintings?

   a. Language

   b. Color and shape

   c. Real objects

   d. Photos

👀 Reading Passage 3

Read the passage and answer questions.

The first group of American landscape painters group emerged in the 1820s and became known as the Hudson River School. It was a group of painters led by Thomas Cole. Many of them painted in and around the Hudson River Valley and also in the newly opened West of America. They described and depicted native scenery of America's wilderness.

The works of Hudson River School were influenced by seventeen-century European landscapes. ***They*** were characterized by panoramic view drawn with precise detail. These panoramic views of nature were intended to evoke noble thoughts and feelings. Indeed, the native wilderness and limitless expanse of continent symbolized nation's potential for greatness. They used light effects and dramatically portrayed such elements as mist and sunset.

1. The word "They" in the passage refers to

    a. American landscape painters

    b. Seventeenth-century Europeans

    c. The works of the Hudson River School

    d. Artists of the Hudson River School

2. What was the main subject of the paintings of the Hudson River School?

    a. People around the Hudson River

    b. Landscape around the school

    c. Native scenes of nature

    d. Thoughts and feelings

Actual Mini TOEFL

After reading the passage, answer questions.

Fauvism was extremely short-lived art style in modern painting, but it was an extremely *important* as well. The style lasted only four years, beginning in 1905. Fauvism is French for "wild beasts." It got this name because paintings had bright and unusual colors. The subjects in paintings were shown in a simple way, and the colors and patterns were bright and wild.

Fauvism officially began with an art exhibition at the Paris Autumn Salon. The artists including Henri Matisse and George Braque gathered *there* to exhibit their newest works.

The leader of this movement was Henri Matisse. While Matisse may not have considered himself a fauvist for a while, he always <u>acknowledged</u> *the movement's importance. "Fauvism isn't everything." He said, "but it is the foundation of everything."* For over 60 years, he created artwork that would become appreciated and admired in museums and collections throughout the world. He is considered one of this century's greatest art masters, like Claude Monnet, Vincent Van Gogh, and Pablo Picasso. His work and ***personality*** have become nearly as bright and brilliant like the word fauvism.

1. What is the main topic of the passage?

    a. The importance of fauvism

    b. A description of fauvism

    c. Fauvism and its representative artist

    d. Henri Matisse's contribution to fauvism

2. The word "important" in the passage is opposite in meaning to

    a. negligible

    b. excessive

    c. ultimate

    d. radical

3. The word "there" in the passage

   refers to

    a. France

    b. an exhibition

    c. their paintings

    d. the movement

4. where does word "fauvism" come from?

   a. Its bright color

   b. Its simple drawing technique

   c. Its representative artist

   d. Its first exhibition

5. The word "acknowledged" in the passage is closest in meaning to

   a. focused

   b. recognized

   c. neglected

   d. announced

6. The word "it" in the passage refers to?

   _____

7. The word "personality" in the passage is closest in meaning to

    a. character

    b. privacy

    c. poverty

    d. history

8. Which of the following is not true about Henri Matisse?

    a. He was a fauvist.

    b. He regarded fauvism as the foundation of everything.

    c. He was always gloomy and pessimistic.

    d. His artwork became famous.

15

Environment on the Earth

15 Environment on the Earth

I **Choose the fact that can be inferred from the passage.**

There are many types of gases in the earth's atmosphere known as greenhouse gases. These include water vapor and carbon dioxide. These greenhouse gases trap

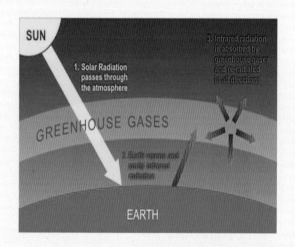

some of the energy from the sun. This keeps heat on the earth in the same way a greenhouse keeps heat and helps the plants inside grow. Without this "greenhouse effect," temperatures on the earth would be too low and living things would not exist.

a. Green gases enable animals and plants to live on the earth.

b. The temperature of the earth is much lower than that of a greenhouse.

c. Many new forms of life are created from greenhouse gases.

II **Read the passage and draw O if the following statements can be inferred and draw X if they cannot.**

The greatest source of pollution in the United States is industry. More than half of all water pollution comes from manufacturing facilities. There are 370,000 facilities

that produce many kinds of waste. The waste is washed into streams, lakes, and oceans. In 1996, the United States Environment Protection Agency reported that about 40% of the nation's water bodies were too polluted to drink or to fish in. They have poisonous chemicals. Even swimming in the water may be dangerous.

a. Fish from polluted waters contain chemicals. ___

b. It is safe to swim in the polluted water. ___

c. The United States researches environmental conditions. ___

😊 Reading Passage 1

Read the passage and answer questions.

Ever since the Industrial Revolution began, fossil fuel such as coal and petroleum has been used to make trucks and cars run, heat homes and businesses, and give power to  factories. The increase in fossil fuel use caused carbon dioxide to increase by 30%, methane more than doubled, and nitrous oxide to increase by 15% in the atmosphere. In addition, it improved heat-trapping capability of the earth.

The result of increasing fossil fuel lead to an increase in the global surface temperature. Since the 19th century, the temperature on the earth has risen by 0.5 to 1.0 degree Fahrenheit. In the 20th century, ten of the warmest years passed in the last 15 years of the century. Higher temperature made ice melt and the melting ice made the global sea level higher. This phenomenon has caused flooding in many parts of the earth.

1. It can be inferred from the passage that

   a. the industrial revolution caused the earth to become warmer.

   b. the 19th century was the warmest century on the earth.

   c. all flooding on the earth is caused by rising temperature.

   d. fossil fuel is being used up around the world.

2. Which of the following is not a gas that has increased after the Industrial Revolution?

   a. Methane

   b. Carbon dioxide

   c. Oxygen

   d. Nitrous oxide

👁 Reading Passage 2

Read the passage and answer questions.

The coastal and inland waters of the earth are getting more and more polluted by large and small boats. These boats regularly dump sewage into the waters. Sometimes, accidents

such as oil spills happen. Oil spills kill birds, fish, and plants. In 1989, the tanker Exon Valdez spilled 11 million gallons of oil in the sea near Alaska. It was one of the worst oil spills. The year before, 22 oil spills occurred.

Oil spills can be dangerous to human life. When pesticides are sprayed to kill insects and rats, the poison called DDT flows in the waters and it is absorbed into the oil that is spilled. Therefore fish and other wildlife in the waters polluted by oil takes in the DDT. If people eat these fish and animals, they also absorbed the DDT. DDT can affect the reproductive power of humans, making them have fewer babies.

1. Which of the following can be inferred from the passage?

    a. More oil was spilled in the past 15 years than at any other time.

    b. DDT is a poisonous substance found in oil.

    c. In 1989, many fish died in the sea near Alaska.

    d. Oil spills occur every year.

2. Which of the following is not a way that humans are polluting the earth?

    a. Throwing waste into the sea

    b. Spraying plants with pesticides

    c. Spilling oil into the earth's water bodies

    d. Eating fish that has swallowed DDT

Reading Passage 3

Read the passage and answer questions.

The world's demand for power and raw materials has been increasing. Since the beginning of 1900s, the use of energy is doubled every twenty years. If humans continue to use the earth's

natural resources at that rate, it is unavoidable that eventually these resources will become exhausted.

One of those that consume the most power in the earth is the computer. Every year, computer sales increased by ten percent. In the end of year 2002, there were one billion computers on the earth and one sixths of the world's population could posses their own computers. There are now enough computers on the earth for every man, woman, and child. To make just one computer requires an incredible amount of fossil fuel and chemicals. But humans throw away their computers easily and buy the newest ones. The discarded computers represent a serious waste of the earth's natural resources.

1. It can be inferred from the passage that

    a. every man, woman, and child on the earth has a computer.

    b. computer industry is not beneficial for the natural resources.

    c. computers caused the world's pollution.

    d. by the end of 21th century, the earth's resources will be used up.

2. All of the following are true except

    a. People liked the used computers more than the new ones.

    b. Much fossil fuel is needed to make one computer.

    c. In the future, any natural resources may not remain.

    d. Much power is used to work on computers.

Actual Mini *TOEFL*

Read the following passage and answer questions.

Although manufacturing and chemical plants are most serious causes of water pollution, the people in towns are also major sources. People living in cities uses a lot of detergent, paper, and

plastic. They also take various drugs and eliminate waste matter from their bodies. The wastes produced in city life are dumped under the ground for disposal. ___(A) The wastes often reached the underground water table, which is ground that has a lot of water. ___ (B) Chemicals and medicinal ingredients from the wastes pollute the underground water. ___(C) Thus, the health of the people living in towns and cities is threaten by the *contaminated* water.

___(D) Another major water polluting source is rain. The rain itself may not be dirty. But the streets and highways are dirty. *They* are coated with highway debris and chemicals from oil and gas used in cars and trucks. The debris and chemicals are *transported* into rivers or seas by the rain. Other types of matter that the rain washes often contain antibiotics and other chemicals used in raising livestock.

1. What is the main topic of the passage?

    a. Acid rain

    b. Water transport system in cities

    c. How wastes are produced

    d. Ways that water becomes contaminated

2. All of the following are sources of water contamination in cities except

    a. pesticides

    b. detergent

    c. medicines that people take

    d. plastic and paper

3. What can be inferred about drinking water from the passage?

    a. There is a plenty of drinking water underground.

    b. Water from faucets is clean enough to drink.

    c. City people are polluting the water they will drink.

    d. It is better to drink ocean water.

4. The following sentence can be added to

> Many people in cities use the polluted water
> for drinking or washing.

5. The word "contaminated" in the passage is closest in meaning to

    a. polluted

    b. contained

    c. terminated

    d. abolished

6. The word "They" in the passage refers to

    a. Polluting source

    b. Streets and highways

    c. Cars and trucks

    d. Towns and cities

7. According to the passage, how does the rain pollute the water?

    a. By being used for drinking in farms

    b. By washing street chemicals into rivers

    c. By the particles contained in rain

    d. By being used in manufacturing plants

8. The word "transported" in the passage is closest in meaning to

    a. evaporated

    b. stored

    c. carried

    d. reduced

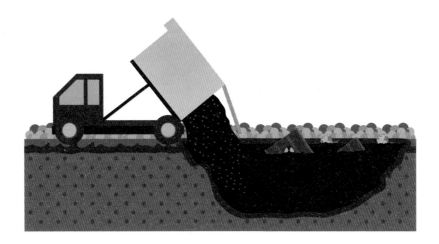

편저자 소개

신봉수

Temple University, 고려대학교 [문학박사, 영어교수법(TESOL) 전공]

(전) 고려대학교, 한국교원대학교, 충남대학교 시간강사
(전) 위덕대학교 영문과 교수
(전) 위덕대학교 입학, 학생처장

Senior Researcher & Visiting Professor
at Bilingual Research Centre of McMaster University (Canada)

저서: 영어교육입문 (서울: 박영사)
　　　영어교육의 이론과 실제 (위덕대학교 출판부)

McMaster English _ Advanced Reading

초판1쇄 인쇄 2019년 5월 10일
초판1쇄 발행 2019년 5월 15일

편저자　　신 봉 수
펴낸이　　임 순 재

펴낸곳　　(주)한올출판사
등　록　　제11-403호
주　소　　서울시 마포구 모래내로 83(성산동, 한올빌딩 3층)
전　화　　(02)376-4298(대표)
팩　스　　(02)302-8073
홈페이지　www.hanol.co.kr
e-메일　　hanol@hanol.co.kr
ISBN 979-11-5685-773-0